SCHIRMER'S LIBRARY
OF MUSICAL CLASSICS

Vol. 2085

ARAM KHACHATURIAN

Selected Piano Works

Intermediate to Early Advanced Level

ISBN 978-1-4234-9020-3

G. SCHIRMER, Inc.

DISTRIBUTED BY

HAL•LEONARD®
CORPORATION
7777 W. BLUEMOUND RD. P.O. BOX 13819 MILWAUKEE, WI 53213

www.schirmer.com
www.halleonard.com

Aram Khachaturian
(1903–1978)

Aram Ilich Khachaturian was born near Tiflis on June 6, 1903 and died in Moscow on May 1, 1978. Educated at the Gnesin School and the Moscow Conservatory, Khachaturian emerged — along with Prokofiev and Shostakovich — as one of the most popular and successful composers of the Soviet period. His unique musical idiom was indelibly marked by his Armenian heritage; his scores are noted for their sensuous, singing melodic writing, colorful orchestration, and elemental rhythmic drive. Known in the West chiefly as the composer of instrumental concertos and the vivid scores for the ballets *Gayaneh* and *Spartacus* (the former including the brilliant "Sabre Dance"), his output also encompassed symphonies and other works for orchestra, film and theater music, works for band, chamber music, and a large number of patriotic and popular songs.

CONTENTS

Adventures of Ivan

2	1. Ivan Sings
4	2. Ivan Can't Go Out Today
7	3. Ivan is Ill
9	4. Ivan Goes to a Party
13	5. Ivan is Very Busy
16	6. Ivan and Natasha
18	7. Ivan's Hobbyhorse
21	8. A Tale of Strange Lands

25	Gayaneh's Dance

28	Fugue

Ten Pieces for The Young Pianist

31	1. On the Trampoline
32	2. Bedtime Story
33	3. Eastern Dance
36	4. The Leopard on the Seesaw
38	5. Snare Drum
41	6. Two Gossiping Old Women
44	7. Funeral March
46	8. Rhythmic Gymnastics
49	9. Toccata
55	10. Fugue

58	Sabre Dance from *Gayaneh*

ADVENTURES OF IVAN

1.
Ivan Sings

Aram Khachaturian (1926–47)
Edited by Alfred Mirovitch

This simple melodious composition is a valuable study for fine syncopated pedal. Never release pedal by fast jerking motion; the movement of the foot should be slow and deliberate.

2.
Ivan Can't Go Out Today

5

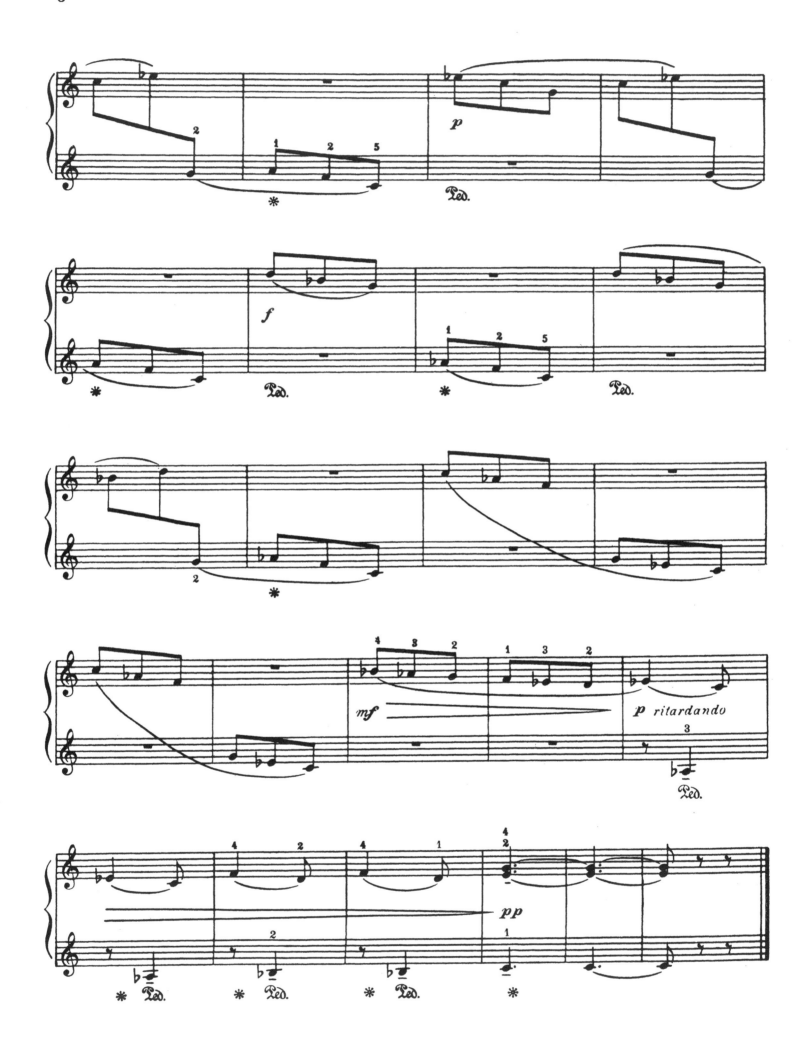

3.
Ivan is Ill

A sustained legato tone quality must be obtained in the heavy sonorous chords in the right hand as well as in the monotonous rising and falling figure in the left hand. Carefully syncopate pedal as indicated.

4.
Ivan Goes to a Party
Waltz

This original and rather humorous little *Waltz* must be light and graceful. To achieve this effect play all accompanying figures in the left hand, as well as in the right, *pp*—"flutteringly". Pedal only as marked.

5.
Ivan is Very Busy

Perfect time and rhythm are essential in this brilliant number. The staccato figure in the left hand should be sharp, short, yet delicate throughout.

6.
Ivan and Natasha

Tempo I

7.
Ivan's Hobbyhorse

8.
A Tale of Strange Lands

23

GAYANEH'S DANCE

Aram Khachaturian

FUGUE

TEN PIECES FOR THE YOUNG PIANIST

1.
On the Trampoline

Aram Khachaturian (1965)

2.
Bedtime Story

3.
Eastern Dance

4.
The Leopard on the Seesaw

5.
Snare Drum

6.
Two Gossiping Old Women

sempre staccato

7.
Funeral March

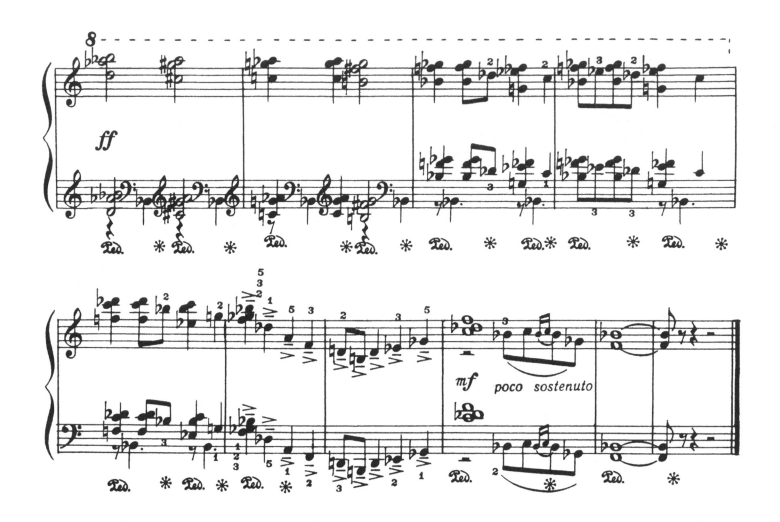

8.
Rhythmic Gymnastics

9.
Toccata

10.
Fugue

SABRE DANCE

from *Gayaneh*

Aram Khachaturian
Arranged by Lawrence Rosen